LEVELS
OF ASSESSMENT

From the Student to the Institution

BY ROSS MILLER AND ANDREA LESKES

PUBLICATIONS IN AAC&U's GREATER EXPECTATIONS SERIES

Greater Expectations: A New Vision for Learning as Nation Goes to College (2002)

Taking Responsibility for the Quality of the Baccalaureate Degree (2004)

The Art and Science of Assessing General Education Outcomes, by Andrea Leskes and Barbara D. Wright (2005)

General Education: A Self-Study Guide for Review and Assessment, by Andrea Leskes and Ross Miller (2005)

General Education and Student Transfer: Fostering Intentionality and Coherence in State Systems,
     edited by Robert Shoenberg (2005)

Levels of Assessment: From the Student to the Institution, by Ross Miller and Andrea Leskes

OTHER RECENT AAC&U PUBLICATIONS ON GENERAL EDUCATION AND ASSESSMENT

Creating Shared Responsibility for General Education and Assessment, special issue of *Peer Review,*
     edited by David Tritelli (Fall 2004)

General Education and the Assessment Reform Agenda, by Peter Ewell (2004)

Our Students' Best Work: A Framework for Accountability Worthy of Our Mission (2004)

Advancing Liberal Education: Assessment Practices on Campus, by Michael Ferguson (2005)

 *Association
of American
Colleges and
Universities*

1818 R Street, NW, Washington, DC 20009-1604

Copyright © 2005 by the Association of American Colleges and Universities.
All rights reserved.

ISBN 0-9763576-6-6

To order additional copies of this publication or to find out about other AAC&U
publications, visit www.aacu.org, e-mail pub_desk@aacu.org, or call 202.387.3760.

This publication was made possible by a grant from Carnegie Corporation of New York.
The statements made and views expressed are solely the responsibility of the authors.

Contents

Introduction

ASSESSMENT CAN ANSWER IMPORTANT QUESTIONS, questions about the learning of individual students, the effectiveness of a single course or program, or even the entire institution. Precision in formulating the questions of interest helps to pinpoint the level of analysis, determine the appropriate methods, and guide data sampling, aggregation, interpretation, and use.

This short paper describes five levels of complexity in assessment at the college level. It was written to help clarify the all-too-common "assessment morass," where questions are left unstated, levels of analysis conflated, and evidence inappropriately gathered.

Our basic assumption is that evidence of student learning should be used for multiple levels of assessment, and we limit our comments here to such evidence. Campuses do, of course, also gather and use information less directly linked to student learning (e.g., related to teaching loads or facilities) and factor it into complex analyses of the learning environment, especially at the program and institutional levels.

The best evidence of learning comes from direct observation of student work rather than from an input inventory (e.g., list of courses completed) or summary of self reports. The student work observed can be either required for a course (embedded) or requested in another context such as a testing situation. Course-embedded assignments provide the *most valid evidence for all levels of analysis* because they are closely aligned with faculty expectations and with the teaching-learning process. The ways of sampling, aggregating, and grouping the evidence for analysis (to make collection more manageable) will depend on the original questions posed. The questions will also determine how the data are interpreted to produce action. Internally, faculty members and staff accomplish aggregation by describing standards, translating them into consistent scoring scales, and anonymously applying the resulting rubrics to the evidence at hand. Such a process does not assign a grade to an individual student but rather attempts to understand better the learning process and how to improve its effectiveness. External assessment tools (e.g., commercial tests) aggregate results by cohort or institutions.

The Art and Science of Assessing General Education Outcomes (Leskes and Wright 2005) and *General Education: A Self-Study Guide for Review and Assessment* (Leskes and Miller 2005), both recently released by the Association of American Colleges and Universities (AAC&U) as part of its Greater Expectations initiative, complement this short paper. Additional resources can be found on the AAC&U Web site (www.aacu.org) and on pages 13 and 14. ■

Level 1. Assessing individual student learning within courses

FORMATIVE AND SUMMATIVE QUESTIONS would probe what individual students are learning and how well they are meeting the goals of a course (whether related to disciplinary content or to using transferable intellectual and practical skills).

Typical assessment questions at this level:

- Is the student learning as expected?

- Has the student's work improved over the semester?

- How well has the student achieved the learning outcomes set for the course?

- What are the student's strengths and weaknesses?

- How well is the instructor communicating with and engaging the student?

Sources of evidence: All student work embedded in the course (for example quizzes and exams, papers, projects, presentations, and portfolios) can provide evidence. This is the level of assessment at which instructor-assigned grades typically provide feedback to students about their progress and success.

Aggregation of data: Aggregation is often sequential as evidence is collected for each student during the course to track individual learning and improvement. Typically a final course grade holistically sums up a semester of learning.

Data uses:

- as formative and/or summative feedback to students so they can understand their progress in the course and ways to improve learning

- for feedback to the course instructor on how well he or she is communicating with and motivating each student (can shape subsequent lessons and assignments within the course)

Responsibilities: Individual students are responsible for the effort they exert, the quality of their work, and meeting the instructor's expectations. They are more likely to fulfill these responsibilities when consistently informed of learning goals and academic norms. By teaching students how to conduct self- and peer-assessments, the professor can improve student understanding of the learning process.

Individual instructors are responsible for setting expectations and making them transparent to students. As educators, their professional responsibility extends to the quality of their own teaching and to monitoring how well the pedagogical methods they employ assist students in learning. While the holistic assignment of grades (an A, B, or F) is a way to evaluate student work, such grades represent averaged estimates of overall quality and communicate little to students about their strengths, weaknesses, or ways to improve. A better way to aid learning is through analytical assessments, which can be as simple as written comments on student papers or as structured as the use of a detailed rubric for an assignment; such analysis can reveal precisely which concepts a student finds challenging. ■

ASSESSING INDIVIDUAL STUDENT LEARNING IN A COURSE

Anne Phillips, professor of Engli at **Kansas State University**, prepares a detailed rubric so students understand the element of an "A" paper. She defines wha she means by

- an interesting thesis (results from thought and judgment)
- useful organization (provides plan for proving the thesis)
- rich detail (includes colorful examples)
- helpful paragraphing (introductory paragraph engages the reader)
- polished mechanics (smooth connects sentences)

Her students can use the rubric to self- or peer-assess their writing as well as to strive toward improvement.

Level 2. Assessing individual student learning across courses

FORMATIVE AND SUMMATIVE QUESTIONS would probe what and how well individual students are learning during the progression of a particular program (e.g., the major, general education) or over their years at college.

Typical assessment questions at this level:

- Has the student's work improved and/or met standards during the program or since admission to college?

- How well has the student achieved the disciplinary outcomes of the major program?

- How well has the student achieved the general learning outcomes of the institution across four years?

Sources of evidence:

- embedded work in individual courses, for example quizzes and exams, papers, projects, presentations

- portfolios that assemble samples of the student's work in a number of courses

- capstone experiences or projects

- student self-reflection on the learning process

- relevant externally developed exams (e.g., for licensure)

Typical grades can provide some holistic feedback to the student but are difficult to interpret across courses except at very broad levels (such as a GPA) or to disaggregate into learning outcomes (e.g., how the student has learned to communicate orally).

Aggregation of data: Given appropriate formats and data, students can aggregate evidence of their own learning (e.g., of a particular skill such as writing) across courses, programs, or their entire time in college to track improvement. Traditionally, departments aggregate an individual's grades across courses when they require, for example, that their majors must maintain a minimum GPA of 2.5 in disciplinary courses.

Data uses:

- as formative and/or summative feedback to students so they can understand their progress over time and ways to improve learning

- for feedback to program faculty on how well individual students are achieving the goals and outcomes

Responsibilities: Individual students are responsible for the quality of their work and for gathering evidence of their learning. They are also responsible for integrating their learning over time and across courses. *Collectively* faculty members share the responsibility for clarifying goals and outcomes and providing rubrics for student self assessment. *Individually* faculty members are responsible for objectively assessing the assembled work samples or the test results and providing both holistic and analytic feedback to the student. ■

ASSESSING INDIVIDUAL STUDENT LEARNING ACROSS COURSES

The teacher education program a **Alverno College** asks students to demonstrate their readiness fc student teaching by showing ho well they perform in certain abili areas (e.g., conceptualization, communication, integration). Using common frameworks and clear expectations, students create portfolios that include lesson plans, a critique of a videotaped lesson, and self assessments. An educational professional from the local P-12 system critiques the portfolio as do department faculty members.

Level 3. Assessing courses

FORMATIVE OR SUMMATIVE QUESTIONS address the achievements of an entire class or the effectiveness of individual or multiple-section courses.

Typical assessment questions at this level:

■ How well is the class collectively achieving the course's content outcomes and objectives (at any one point, at the end)? How well is the class collectively achieving general or transferable learning outcomes and objectives?

■ Are the assignments helping students achieve the expected level of knowledge or skills?

■ How well are students prepared for the following courses in the sequence?

■ Is the course level appropriately targeted for the ability(ies) of the students when they begin?

■ With what degree of consistency do different sections of a course achieve similar outcomes?

■ How well is the course fulfilling its purpose in a larger curriculum?

Sources of evidence:

■ embedded assignments of students in the course (papers, exams, projects, journals, portfolios)

■ externally or commercially developed tests, as long as they are well aligned with the teaching and learning of the course

■ course portfolios constructed by the instructor that include syllabi, expectations, and examples of student work

■ for multi-section courses, common assignments that provide evidence across sections

At the course level, traditional holistic student grades are unlikely to provide sufficiently detailed insights to answer the questions unless tightly tied to explicit analytical standards and scoring rubrics.

Aggregation of data:

- *To assess individual courses:* Sampling the work of all students in a course can reveal how well the course content and assignments are helping students achieve the expected outcomes.

- *To assess multi-section courses:* Common assignments across sections (or common requirements such as a student or course portfolio) can be sampled, averaged, compared, discussed, or otherwise reviewed by the faculty involved and/or by departments or committees to ensure consistency across sections.

- *To assess both individual courses and multi-section courses:* Student portfolios and end-of-course reflections can provide evidence of both cognitive and affective learning outcomes aggregated at the level of the individual student.

Data uses:

- for formative feedback so instructors can improve learning

- for summative feedback to inform planning for the future by an instructor or a course committee

- to support cross-sectional analysis of how consistently multi-section courses are achieving important learning outcomes or the purposes of the course in a sequence

Responsibilities: Instructors and committees are responsible for setting expectations for the course, establishing common standards for multi-section courses, understanding how the course fits into a coherent pathway of learning, and using analysis of the evidence to improve teaching and course design. ■

USING STUDENT LEARNING TO ASSESS A COURSE

At **Binghamton University**, for course to be included in a general education category the instructor must agree to certain guidelines established by the faculty senate. To assess the course, the oversight committee asks the faculty member for a course portfolio that includes examples of student work representing high quality, average, and unacceptable achievement. Guided by approved criteria, an assessment team reviews the course portfolio in relation to the desired goals for student learning. The data gathered are used to determine how well courses satisfy the learning outcomes for each category; they can be further aggregated to examine the category as a whole.

Level 4. Assessing Programs

SOME FORMATIVE BUT MOSTLY SUMMATIVE QUESTIONS guide assessment of programs (e.g., general education or a major).

Typical assessment questions at this level:

- Do the program's courses, individually and collectively, contribute to its outcomes as planned?

- How well does the program fulfill its purposes in the entire curriculum?

- How well do the program's sub-categories (e.g., distributive requirements in general education) contribute to the overall purposes?

- Does the program's design resonate with its expected outcomes?

- Are the courses organized in a coherent manner to allow for cumulative learning?

- Does the program advance institution-wide goals as planned?

Sources of evidence: Direct evidence of student learning from many sources can contribute to program-level assessment: assignments from individual courses, student portfolios built over the program's duration, entering student tests or assignments, capstone projects, results of common assignments, commercial tests. Selected assignments from other programs can be re-scored (given a "second reading") by program faculty (e.g., to assess the general education program's success in developing such institution-wide goals as communication, quantitative literacy, critical thinking, or ethical responsibility). Given the number of potential data sources and the amount of evidence that could be amassed, careful planning is needed to identify the important points for sampling and analysis. Program assessment may likely involve several sources of evidence gathered at the point of entry, a midpoint, and at the end of the program. End point data is particularly valuable as a summative indicator of how well the program, taken as a whole, is achieving its goals. Individual student grades are not informative at this level.

Aggregation of data: Course-level assessments of the courses in a program can be analyzed individually or collectively to reveal whether program goals are being achieved; sampling might be prudent in a large program. Information about the sub-categories in a program (e.g., distribution areas) can be aggregated to the program level (e.g., general education). Sampling of student portfolios considered excellent, average, and sub-par can vividly portray growth in student performance from beginning to the end of a program. Disaggregated data can reveal how sub-groups of students are succeeding in the program. Some external, commercially available assessments can be compared to norms (e.g., the Major Field Tests from ETS).

Data uses:

- to confirm the purpose of the program (e.g., its place in the entire curriculum or connection to mission)

- to check alignment of program design with program outcomes

- to discern how well the program, from its beginning to end, fosters cumulative learning of the desired outcomes

- to discover how well the program as a whole enables students to achieve end-point levels of competence for all program outcomes

- to identify superfluous and/or missing curricular and co-curricular elements in the program

Responsibilities: Responsibility largely rests on the program faculty, *collectively* and *individually*. Collectively, the faculty assumes responsibility for the entire program achieving its—and relevant institution-wide—goals and outcomes. Individual instructors are responsible for advancing the program and institutional goals embedded in their courses. Faculty members cooperate in establishing program "standards" and scoring rubrics for the quality of work expected. ■

USING STUDENT LEARNING TO ASSESS A PROGRAM

At **Buffalo State University**, the general education program is built on student learning in twelve areas, nine discipline- and three skill-based. A complete cycle of assessment occurs over three years with four areas assessed each year to provide the program-level picture. Evidence gathered in individual general education courses is compared to detailed statements of learning outcomes and objectives for each area. The faculty members from the relevant departments design the type of work product expected, a range which includes objective exams, common embedded exam questions, assigned papers, and portfolios. The same professors also pick the most appropriate sampling method and set assessment standards. Evidence aggregated by skill or disciplinary area is then analyzed and discussed by the departments, leading to changes in the program when necessary.

Level 5. Assessing the institution

INSTITUTION-LEVEL ASSESSMENT can be undertaken for internal improvement or to meet external accountability demands. Results of the former can often also serve the latter purpose.

Typical assessment questions at this level:

- What do the institution's educational programs add up to in terms of student learning?

- How well are the institution's goals and outcomes for student learning being achieved?

- How much have our students learned over their college years?

- How well does the institution educate students for the complexities of the twenty-first century?

- What evidence is there that the institution is fulfilling its educational mission?

- How can institutional effectiveness be demonstrated authentically to external stakeholders?

Sources of evidence: A significant body of evidence from multiple sources will be required to answer institution-level questions. Documentation of how well students are meeting institution-wide goals and outcomes requires a clear statement of these learning expectations. The picture of student learning will be based primarily on summarized data from program assessments, supplemented by results from appropriate exams (such as those taken for graduate or professional school admissions, licensure, or certification). Sampling student work, both at the entry- and graduation-levels, can serve to answer value-added assessment questions. Some selected course-level assessments—particularly from common experience courses such as a required core—could contribute to the institution-wide picture. Indirect measures of student learning (National Study of Student Engagement [NSSE], Cooperative Institutional Research Program [CIRP], etc.) may also be informative at this level but should be considered as supplementary to the direct measures.

Aggregation of data: Much of the data will already have been aggregated when analyzed for institutional-level assessment: aggregated by courses, by programs, or by student cohort. For example, sampled, aggregated, and summarized student achievement of the desired learning outcomes in a freshman general education course could be compared to sampled, aggregated, and summarized achievement in a senior capstone. Or an analysis of the cohort completing the Collegiate Learning Assessment instrument could reveal the level of critical thinking in the graduating class. Constructing both narrative and quantitative summaries of the "stories" from programs will shape the broad picture of teaching and learning at the institution. Disaggregated data can reveal how well sub-groups of students are succeeding.

Data uses:

- to reveal what students know and can do when they graduate in order to guide the design of the institution's undergraduate program

- to understand the value added by an institution's undergraduate program

- to discover the interactions among various programs (e.g., general education and the majors), especially in how they help students achieve institution-wide learning goals

- to guide and support decisions about resource allocation, faculty hiring, and professional development

- to demonstrate to external stakeholders the institution's effectiveness in educating students

Responsibilities: The responsibility for institution-level assessment rests with administrators working in close collaboration with the faculty, student affairs professionals, and other campus staff members. Collaborative groups would design an ongoing comprehensive program of institutional assessment, use data to improve learning, keep student success a top priority, ensure linkages to strategic planning and resource allocation, and communicate with external groups. ∎

USING STUDENT LEARNING TO ASSESS AN INSTITUTION

Truman State University use variety of instruments—some developed internally and others externally—for comprehensive institution-level assessment. Dire measures of performance includ portfolio compiled by seniors, th nationally normed Academic Pro test for juniors, writing samples from a writing-across-the-university program, senior capstones, and standardized ser tests in the major (e.g., GRE and GMAT). This direct evidence is complemented by indirect measures (such as CIRP for freshmen, NSSE for freshmen ar seniors, and alumni surveys). In addition to contributing to the institutional profile, some results are made available by discipline or division.

References

Leskes, Andrea, and Ross Miller. 2005. *General education: A self-study guide for review and assessment.* Washington, DC: Association of American Colleges and Universities.

Leskes, Andrea, and Barbara D. Wright. 2005. *The art and science of assessing general education outcomes.* Washington, DC: Association of American Colleges and Universities.

Web Resources

On individual student-level assessment

Individual student learning within courses

depts.alverno.edu/saal/essentials.html

Gateway to information about Alverno College's rich assessment practices

ustudies.semo.edu/oralcom/holistic.htm

An oral presentation holistic scoring rubric from Southeast Missouri State University

www.flaguide.org

Gateway to Field-tested Learning Assessment Guide (FLAG) and multiple assessment resources in science, mathematics, engineering, and technology

www.k-state.edu/assessment/Learning/APaper.pdf

Five Characteristics of an A Paper—a scoring guide for writing from Kansas State University

www.uas.alaska.edu/humanities/documents/j-sp-comp-assess.pdf

Eight public speaking competencies and criteria for assessment from the University of Alaska Southeast

Individual student learning across courses

kings.edu/academics/capprogram.htm

King's College assessment information—especially the sections on the "sophomore-junior diagnostic project" and the "senior integrated assessment"

www.wvsctc.edu/InstitutionalEffectiveness/Self-Study%20Attachments.pdf

See page 115 of West Virginia Sate Community and Technical College's self-study for a student portfolio assessment rubric

On course-level assessment

provost.binghamton.edu/policy.html

Click on the link to "Assessment of General Education at Binghamton University: Program and Guidelines" for course assessment guidelines

www.bgsu.edu/offices/provost/academicprograms/genedprogram/Embedded%20assessment.htm

Course-level assessment at Bowling Green State University using course-embedded assessment to gather data

On program-level assessment

web.bsu.edu/IRAA/AA/WB/contents.htm

An assessment workbook from Ball State University

www.buffalostate.edu/offices/assessment/gened.htm

General education program assessment at Buffalo State University. Also major program assessment at www.buffalostate.edu/offices/assessment/majorprogram.htm

www.calstatela.edu/academic/aa/ugs/geassess/geplan.htm

Assessment plan for general education, California State University, Los Angeles

www.ets.org/portal/site/ets/menuitem.htm

ETS link to standardized tests, some appropriate for general education—see especially MAPP

www.sinclair.edu/about/gened/reports/assessment/index.cfm

Assessment of General Education at Sinclair Community College

On institution-level assessment

assessment.truman.edu/components/index.htm

Truman State University, a leader in assessment, describes the components of a comprehensive assessment program

assessment.umflint.edu/GeneralEducation/

Documents from University of Michigan, Flint clarify that general education goals are developed throughout a student's time at the university, not only during study in the general education program

On multiple levels of assessment

depts.alverno.edu/ere/index.html

Multiple links to Alverno College's well-developed systems of assessment

www.ets.org

Select "Resources for Higher Education"

www.stanford.edu/group/ncpi/unspecified/toolkits.shtml

National Center for Postsecondary Improvement at Stanford University assessment toolkits (Improving Student Assessment, Engagement in Assessment, and State Government and Regional Accreditation Association Policies for Assessment of Student Learning: Tools for Policymakers and Administrators, among others)

www.winthrop.edu/acad_aff/GenEd/NewGenEdProgram.htm

Winthrop University document linked to detailed descriptions of outcomes and assessments

Note: All Web addresses current as of publication date.

Print Resources

Gaff, Jerry G., James L. Ratcliff, et al. 1997. *Handbook of the undergraduate curriculum*. San Francisco: Jossey-Bass.
In particular Part Five: Administration and assessment of the curriculum

Maki, Peggy L. 2004. *Assessing for learning: Building a sustainable commitment across the institution*. Sterling, VA: Stylus.
Primarily institution-level and program-level assessment

Middle States Commission on Higher Education. 2003. *Student learning assessment: Options and resources*. Philadelphia: Middle States Commission on Higher Education.

About the Authors

Ross Miller joined the Association of American Colleges and Universities (AAC&U) in 1999, as director of programs for the Office of Education and Quality Initiatives, to assist in the planning and implementation of the Greater Expectations initiative. He is also assistant director of the AAC&U Institute on General Education.

Miller holds a BM and MM in trumpet performance from the University of Michigan and an EdD in music education from the University of Illinois. During his thirteen years at Nazareth College (Rochester, New York), he taught both undergraduate and graduate music education students while also serving as director of the graduate program. In an assignment as Nazareth's assessment coordinator, Miller was responsible for assessment of the college's general education program. He has served as a question writer in the arts for the National Assessment of Educational Progress and worked on a team developing a high school outcomes test in the arts for the New York State Education Department.

Andrea Leskes, vice president for education and quality initiatives at AAC&U since 1999, led the Greater Expectations initiative on the aims and best practices of undergraduate education for the twenty-first century. The principal author of *Greater Expectations: A New Vision for Learning as a Nation Goes to College,* Leskes also directs AAC&U's annual Institute on General Education, writes regularly for the association's quarterly journals, and consults with campuses on curricular reform.

Leskes holds a PhD in cell biology from the Rockefeller University and an MA in French from the University of Massachusetts at Amherst. She formerly served as vice president for academic affairs and professor of comparative literature at the American University of Paris, vice provost for undergraduate education at Northeastern University, associate dean at Brandeis University, and assistant dean at Dartmouth College. ∎